A WAY WHERE THERE IS NO WAY

(A Guide to the Straight and Narrow)

My Motivation

Ecclesiastes 12:12 "And further, by these, my son, be admonished: of making many books there is no end; and much study is a weariness of the flesh."

In light of this verse, one might wonder why I felt a need to write this book. That's a good question, and one I've asked myself.

My first reason comes from a desire to help bring unity to the body of Christ. In the 17th chapter of John we see Jesus praying for us that we might be one. There is truly a sense in which all believers are one in Christ Jesus, but I don't believe that this fully answers Jesus' prayer. I believe, in these last days, Jesus knows that we need to be united in a more complete way. Differences of opinion have divided the body of Christ over the centuries and previous attempts to bring unity, focused on settling these differences, have most often resulted in greater division. Some doctrines are essential because we cannot believe in things we have not heard. Other doctrines, some of which have

1

divided the church, are only good or bad based on what effect they have on the hearers. It is not my intention to establish new doctrine or tear down old. My only hope is to enhance our abilities to draw closer to God and one another by sharing some of what God has used to accomplish these ends in my life.

Jeremiah 29:11 "For I know the thoughts that I think toward you, saith the Lord, thoughts of peace, and not of evil, to give you an expected end."

Secondly, I am presently over 70 years old and have been walking with God over 40 years. I consider myself to be "OMNI-DENOMINATIONAL", and as such, I embrace all true believers in all denominational and non-denominational groups as brothers and sisters in Christ. I also embrace all others as loved by God our Father and our Lord and Savior Jesus Christ. I believe that God has a plan for each of us and it is my hope that by sharing my experiences we might more easily follow His plan.

Phillippians 1:9-11 "And this I pray, that your love may abound yet more and more in knowledge and in all judgment; that ye may approve things that are excellent; that ye may be sincere and without offence till the day of Christ; being filled with the fruits of righteousness, which are by Jesus Christ, unto the glory and praise of God."

My third and perhaps the greatest reason is my hope that our love for God and for each other would become more abundant and that our lives might bear much fruit unto the glory and praise of God.

A WAY WHERE THERE IS NO WAY

(A Guide to the Straight and Narrow)

Explanation

The first thing I need to do is explain the title of this book. Until we understand that it is impossible for anyone to be saved, we cannot begin to appreciate or understand the grace and mercy of God. Let's look at Matthew 19:23-26, "Then said Jesus unto his disciples, Verily I say unto you, That a rich man shall hardly enter into the kingdom of heaven. And again I say unto you, It is easier for a camel to go through the eye of a needle, than for a rich man to enter into the kingdom of God. When his disciples heard it, they were exceedingly amazed, saying, Who then can be saved? But Jesus beheld them, and said unto them, With men this is impossible; but with God all things are possible."

Notice that Jesus says two things about rich men. First, they will hardly enter into the kingdom and second, that it's impossible. If common sense doesn't tell us that it's impossible for a camel to pass through the eye of a needle, then the reaction of the disciples and Jesus' answer must establish this fact. The disciples broadened the question to

4

include everyone when they said "who then can be saved?" These two things, on the surface, seem contradictory just as my title does. Both things are true. It is absolutely impossible for us to be saved. There is absolutely nothing we can do to save ourselves. Our situation is totally hopeless from our point of view. Thankfully the second part of Jesus' statement is also true. With God all things are possible. We should take a minute to try and wrap our minds around this.

At times I hear people say that some things are impossible for God. I could take time to enumerate some of the things that are thought to be impossible for God, but I'm afraid that would become tedious and boring. Instead, I will answer these in the best way I know. There are two reasons that people believe something is impossible for God. First, we view the problem from our perspective, and perceive God's ability as limited by our own inability. In other words, we do not fully understand the problem or the power of God. Secondly, we forget that all things exist only because God says they exist. God spoke all things into being. When we limit God to our understanding of Him, no matter how good that understanding may be, we underestimate God. One of the biggest mistakes we can make is to limit

God in anything. We can search the gospels and not find one place where Jesus said, "You are believing for too much" but we can find many instances where people are admonished for not believing enough. One of the worst mistakes we can make is to limit God's transforming grace and power in our lives. Henry Ford said "Whether you think you can, or you think you can't – you're right." It is we, ourselves, who limit God's power in our lives through unbelief.   We can do all things through Christ who strengthens us. John 1:12 says. "But as many as received him, to them gave he power to become the sons of God, even to them that believe on his name."

Chapter 1

Getting it Right

This one thing I know! I am wrong about some things. 1 Corinthians 13:12, "For now we see through a glass, darkly; but then face to face: now I know in part; but then shall I know even as also I am known." This is one of the first things God tried to make me aware of. When I was a young Christian my main goals were to get everything right and correct everyone else's errors. I remember the day I first prayed "the sinner's prayer". I also remember the day I prayed that same prayer the second, third and ...times. They were all done on the same day. I prayed that prayer over and over again to be sure I got it right. I was making two mistakes. I thought that the prayer was saving me, and I also thought that if I didn't get it right I might not be saved. We'll talk more about this later when we take a closer look at salvation. I only mention it now so that you'll understand my state of mind when I first heard someone say, "It's not what you know but who you know that saves us." It really rubbed me the wrong way. I had heard that phrase used so often referring to how you get ahead in the world. In spite of that, by the third or fourth time I heard it I began to understand. It has taken about thirty years to really sink in. The apostle Paul, who wrote most of the epistles and spent three years being taught by Jesus after the resurrection, said "We know in part" "We see through a glass darkly". That one word "we" brings two things to mind. If Paul only knew in part, I certainly am wrong about some things and anybody who believes they are not wrong about some things, is certainly wrong about that, and other things besides. The other thing this brings to mind is that all denominations believe some things that are wrong. It doesn't matter who your favorite teacher is, who you look to for spiritual leadership, or what church you go to, some of what you hear will be wrong. I am sure that parts of this book will be wrong. This is my warning to you. Whatever you listen to, or whatever you read, treat it the same way as eating fish. Eat the meat, and spit out the bones. The bones only hurt you when you try to swallow them whole and choke on them.   Chew everything thoroughly and spit out the bones. Part of what I want to do in this book is expose what I feel are bones. These are things that have choked my spiritual growth, and I share them hoping only to help guide you in the way. If you disagree with me, it may be one place where I'm wrong. Chew everything thoroughly and spit out the bones.

One interesting thing about knowing that I'm wrong about some things is this. If I knew what I was wrong about, I would change my mind because I really don't like being wrong about anything. I am sure this holds true for most people. I can't imagine people wanting to be wrong. Given this problem I cannot be one-hundred per-cent sure that if we disagree on something, I am not the one who is wrong. A little of this self-doubt can make us much better listeners. I can't help but think that this can bring us closer together.

Knowing that we are wrong about some things may not seem very important, but I assure you it is far more important than most people realize. If we look at an overview of the gospels we see that Jesus preferred the company of "common people" like fishermen, tax collectors and sinners. In Jesus' day we see two groups of people who thought they had all the answers right. They were called Pharisees and Sadducees. These were the two main denominations spoken of by Jesus. They argued and fought with one another so much that in the book of acts we see them rioting over whether or not there is a resurrection. I can't think of any instances where Jesus said anything good about either group. I think we should take some time to consider this.

For many years I told people that I might be a heretic. A couple of years ago, when I was in Afghanistan, a wonderful friend told me that I should quit doing that for two reasons. The first was because it turns people off to anything I had to say, and the second was because I'm not a heretic. This caused me to look more closely into what a heretic is. The word "heresy" is actually a Greek word that means disunion, party or sect. Because my heart's desire is to see Jesus' prayer in John 17 fully answered, I am probably closer to being a direct opposite to a heretic. I own a book, written by Rulon S. Howells, titled "His Many Mansions", with a comparative chart of ten Christian denominations on twenty-three important doctrinal questions. We might disagree on whether or not all ten of the denominations are Christian or whether all twenty-three doctrinal questions are important, but it breaks my heart that there are divisions among us and according to this chart no two sects seem to fully agree on anything. John 17:20 "Neither pray I for these alone, but for them also which shall believe on me through their word; that they all may be one; as thou, Father, art in me, and I in thee, that they also may be one in us: that the world may believe that thou hast sent me." Can we learn to love one another instead of hunting for specks in each other's eyes?

There is another important reason we need to know that we're wrong about some things. It's interesting what Jesus says in Matthew. "Not every one that saith unto me, Lord, Lord, shall enter into the kingdom of heaven;" and "Then shall the righteous answer him, saying, Lord, when saw we thee an hungered, and fed thee? or thirsty, and gave thee drink?". There seems to be an indication here, at least, that some people who think they have all the answers will not enter into the kingdom of God and some who don't even know what they're doing right will enter. This all makes better sense when you realize the very basis upon which Jesus prays that our sins be forgiven. While hanging on the cross, paying for the sins of all mankind, Jesus prayed this prayer for each one of us. "Then said Jesus, Father, forgive them; for they know not what they do." It's when we think we have it all figured out that we are in the most danger.

There are two questions we need to answer. The first is, "Can the gravity or number of our sins keep us from being forgiven?" and the second is, "How many incorrect doctrines do we need to separate us from God's love and mercy?" The Bible mentions only one sin that cannot be forgiven and that is rejecting our salvation. It is when we are puffed up in our own sight, and believe that we have it all figured out, that we think our brother is a fool and we are in danger of hell fire. Every sin was forgiven when Jesus prayed for us who don't know what we're doing. Foolish and vain questions gender strife, but the humble acceptance of our limitations brings love, understanding and healing to the Body of Christ.

Before I continue it is necessary for me to clarify some things. Oftentimes the difference between good doctrine and bad doctrine is the extent to which it is taken. Taken to the extremes, the things I have said could become bad doctrine. For example, when I pointed out the relationship between the word "heresy" and churches being divided over doctrine it is possible to think that I'm against churches or believe that all churches are founded on heresy. When I pointed out that our doctrines are not one-hundred percent correct we might be tempted to ask ourselves if doctrine is at all important. Obviously I think doctrine (teaching) is important. That is part of what this book is doing. I love the churches and I believe they are wonderful places and are necessary. I believe that most of the leaders in these churches love God and care deeply for their members. I also believe that most people attending these churches are sincere in their faith and improve their relationships with God and one another. Just because doctrine and churches are imperfect does not mean we should throw them out. We live, after all, in an imperfect world. If we reject things because of their imperfection we would have nothing left and sometimes imperfections may even add beauty. God loves us with all of our imperfections and we need to love one another while recognizing our own imperfections.

Chapter 2

The Greatest Day

Earlier I mentioned the day I prayed "the sinner's prayer". This is probably the best place to start because that was the greatest day of my life. In my early life I was blessed to be raised in a Catholic family. I don't remember being baptized as an infant, but I know I was. I attended a Catholic school and was a poor student, but I always did well in religious studies. My mother's family would have been classified as devout Catholics. Some of my earliest memories are sitting at my great grandmother's feet while she was either praying or working. She could have been the woman Proverbs 31 was written about. Her daughter, my grandmother, prayed for me every day of my life until she died when she was over a hundred. The very first miracle I ever saw was when my grandmother prayed for me to be healed from a growth I had on my neck. When she prayed, she anointed my neck with oil she identified as oil of St. Jude. St. Jude, yes the same St. Jude that Danny Thomas talked about, is the patron saint of impossible cases. I don't remember if it happened instantly or not, but by the next day it was gone. I could never have been an agnostic after that. I continued as a Catholic through First Communion and Confirmation. Being so close to two women who most certainly should have been eligible to be canonized Saints in the Catholic Church made me acutely aware of my shortcomings. I believed that a million years in purgatory might just start my punishment, so I sought every indulgence with great zeal. When I was fourteen my parents, who I had never seen argue, committed the unpardonable sin, in the Catholic Church, and got divorced. I'm telling you this so that you'll know that I still love the Catholic Church and the people in it, and why. I am certain that God moves in that Church and that the Church is far from perfect. The more we become like Jesus, the more we will love things in spite of their imperfections.

When my parents divorced my whole life changed. My sister and I became what I refer to as "throw away children" and the good that came out of it was, I began to question everything. At seventeen I joined the Navy because I had been kicked out of my father's house and had nowhere else to go. I tried desperately to consume my share of the world's liquor supply until that prayer changed my life. When I was in boot camp I went forward for salvation, but that was only because you'd have to be crazy to be in the military and not know that

15

you would go to heaven if you died. When I was in the Philippines I joined the local protestant Church of Christ. I remember the preacher asking me if I feared God. I didn't think I had any reason to be afraid of God so I answered no. He told me that I should have said yes and so I did. I only attended that Church a couple of times. My life did not appear to have any significant change from the experience. It wasn't until I was married and had three children that my life was changed.

My wife and I were invited by some of our neighbors to a little party. We didn't know at the time that it was an outreach from a local branch of the Christian and Missionary Alliance Church. The very first thing we noticed was we were able to have fun and not drink. This is something that neither of us had experienced in our adult lives. We began to attend that Church and were almost immediately caught up in the controversy over the "Baptism of the Holy Spirit" with the evidence of "speaking in tongues". At the same time we began attending a home Bible study that was started by an Assembly of God preacher. It was there that salvation was offered to my wife and I, and we prayed that "sinner's prayer". We did not understand much about salvation and we had very little knowledge of the Bible, yet God reached down in the middle of these two denominations divided in controversy and turned our lives around. God used two denominations to transform our lives.

Just as good doctrine can help us in our journey, a good understanding of our salvation can draw us closer to God and help us to interact with one another in love, understanding our flaws and limitations. I certainly, even now, have only a partial understanding of how I was saved, but the understanding I do have has helped me in both those relationships. Because this understanding grows daily, I feel very inadequate as I share this with you but, because it has greatly influenced me for the better, I feel compelled to share it.

God not only knows all things, but He also has always had a plan for each of us. He created Adam in His own image. Adam, like God, was good. God even said it was "very good". In the short version, Adam listened to the devil's lie and for some reason believed that if he could just have a little evil in his life he would be more like God. Instead he changed into a creature ruled by the god of this world (the devil) and the lusts of his own flesh. He freed himself from God to become a god to himself. I do not know how much he resembled

God after that, but all mankind from then on has been born in the image of Adam. Genesis 5: 3 "And Adam lived an hundred and thirty years, and begat a son in his own likeness, after his image."

None of this surprised God. He loves each person with the love that goes way beyond anything we can imagine. Because of that love, He sent Jesus, His only begotten Son, who is the express image of God His Father, into this world to die for our sins. Jesus said, "Father, forgive them for they know not what they do." Jesus prayed this prayer for those who were crucifying Him. Every person who ever sinned was included in that prayer, because Jesus carried all the sins of mankind to that cross. Every person was forgiven of every sin that they have committed when God answered that prayer and proved it by raising Jesus from the dead. This forgiveness is offered freely to everyone and is the very basis for our salvation. When I view our salvation this way I cannot feel superior to anyone because I received forgiveness for my sin because God loves me just like he loves you and there is nothing I ever did to deserve it.

God has a plan for each and every one of us and that plan is motivated by love. Romans 8:29 "For whom he did foreknow, he also did predestinate to be conformed to the image of his Son, that he might be the firstborn among many brethren." and Ephesians 1:5 "having predestinated us unto the adoption of children by Jesus Christ to himself, according to the good pleasure of his will." "God is not willing that any should perish." God's plan for your life (your destiny) is that you be born again into the family of God and be conformed into the image of His Son, Jesus. Hebrews 2:3 "How shall we escape, if we neglect so great salvation?"

According to John's gospel, Nicodemas, a ruler of the Jews, and a Pharisee, came to Jesus one night and, before he could ask a question, Jesus answered "Verily, verily, I say unto thee, Except a man be born again, he cannot see the kingdom of God." Even though Jesus died for our sins and forgave us, we were born in the image of Adam and must be born again into the family of God in order to start being conformed to the image of Jesus. When I was born in the flesh, I didn't have much to do with it. I was there but I don't remember it. I was alive and I was growing. I don't remember any of it. I only know these things because I've seen others born and I know that I was born. I believe I was born of the spirit when I prayed "the sinner's prayer." That is why that day is the most important day of my life. I believe that

God gives everybody enough faith to be born again. Ephesians 2:8 "For by grace are ye saved through faith; and that not of yourselves: it is the gift of God: not of works, lest any man should boast. For we are his workmanship, created in Christ Jesus unto good works, which God hath before ordained that we should walk in them." It is the faith that God gave me that allowed me to be born again. God loves us all the same and gives everyone the faith they need. What we do with that faith is up to us. How can we neglect "so great a salvation"?

Faith comes before action because, whether our actions are good or bad, we always act on what we believe. We always need a reason for doing things. When the reason comes before we act, we have faith our actions will have a desired result. If our reasons come after our actions, they are only excuses. It is because of the faith that God gives us that we pray "the sinner's prayer" or do anything else that pertains to salvation. God's grace comes to us through faith. Even the good works that follow are a result of His grace working in us through that faith. When I view my salvation in this way I find that my love for God grows and I do not elevate myself above others. The more I have in common with people, the better I can relate to them and the easier it is to love them. If God does it all, then even the different churches are but tools in His hands used to mold us to the image of Jesus. This is our destiny.

Chapter 3

Important Things We Can and Cannot Do

The next Church I attended was a United Pentecostal Church. I didn't have to go very far because I had changed my garage into a Church for them. There were some wonderful people in that Church who knew how to pray and worship God. It's the only place I have literally "seen" the Spirit of God move.

One evening after service in my garage/church we were praying for a woman who needed to be delivered from a demon of fear. As we prayed for her, the demon spoke. It said "I'm afraid". We commanded this demon of fear to leave her. After a short time, while we were praying, she turned to a corner of the building and screamed "Jesus." I immediately turned and looked at that corner of the building and saw a somewhat translucent rider on a white horse coming through the wall. I assumed the rider to be Jesus because of the scream "Jesus." Since the horse and rider were going toward the woman we were praying for, my attention was drawn back to her. I saw, what appeared to be, a dark cloud leave her in the opposite direction. She was totally delivered from that point on.

For those of you who are not familiar with the (UPC) United Pentecostal Church's doctrines, I'm going to go over some briefly.   The UPC would be classified, by most of us, as a "holiness church". They have standards of conduct that may differ slightly from one congregation to another. Their ministers cannot be divorced. Women cannot cut their hair. Men must look like men. Women must look like women. Movies and television were forbidden. Women could not wear pants or makeup. These are some of the most common rules. Most of these rules arise from a zealous desire to do God's will and a meticulous study of the Bible. Another doctrine held by this church is called "oneness".   Briefly stated, they believe that Jesus, God the Father, and God the Holy Ghost are one and the same. They base this belief in part on two scriptures. Matthew 28:19 "baptizing them in the name of the Father, and of the Son, and of the Holy Ghost" and, Acts 2:38 "be baptized every one of you in the name of Jesus Christ". They point out that the name is singular and that the terms Father, Son, and Holy Ghost are titles and the apostles responded to this command by always baptizing in Jesus' name.   While this may be viewed as an extremely unified view of God, an extreme view also exists in some denominations regarding the division of God. It's of little wonder that misunderstandings can occur over things we can't possibly fully understand. The third and final doctrine I'm going to mention here is the belief that we must be baptized in Jesus' name to be saved. The necessity for baptism as a requirement for salvation is based primarily on two scriptures, namely Mark 16:16 and Acts 2:38. "He that believeth and is baptized shall be saved; but he that believeth not shall be damned." "Then Peter said unto them, Repent, and be baptized every one of you in the name of Jesus Christ for the remission of sins, and ye shall receive the gift of the Holy Ghost."

In the twenty-third chapter of Luke we have an account of a man's salvation. When Jesus was crucified he had on either side of Him a thief. At first they both mocked Him, but eventually one of them had a change of heart. He began to rebuke the other thief saying, "Dost not thou fear God, seeing thou art in the same condemnation? And we indeed justly; for we receive the due reward of our deeds: but this man hath done nothing amiss.", and he said unto Jesus, "Lord, remember me when thou comest into thy kingdom." Even though this man was a thief he believed in God, and assumed that the other thief also believed in God. He also believed that they both deserved to be crucified. Sometime between the third and ninth hour of that day this man was born again. As a result, his heart was changed. He began to have compassion for Jesus and believed that Jesus could intercede for him. He did the only things he could do in his situation. He took Jesus' side against the other thief and asked Jesus to remember him. He is indeed a wonderful example of what we must do to be saved. He repented of his dead works, confessed that he had sinned and believed in the saving work of Jesus.

It is interesting to notice the things he couldn't do. He could not be baptized because he was hanging on a cross. He couldn't believe all of our "very important" doctrines because there wasn't enough time to go over them all. I don't believe he even had time to think about each and every sin he had committed or confess them. This doesn't mean that these things aren't good or important. Sometimes we can't do things even if they are important. I can't save myself, and that's the most important thing there is. Even though I have repented of dead works, I find that sin raises its ugly head again and again. I'm sure there are sins in my life that I am not aware of. I know that I shouldn't lie and yet at times I fool myself. We need to do all we can and trust God to make a way for us where there is no way. As people, it sometimes seems easy to lay down a bunch of rules and make a list of dos and don'ts, but I thank God that His mercy endures forever, and salvation is of the Lord.

It seems to me that our focus should be more on things we can do than on the things we can't. In 1st Corinthians chapter 13 Paul says something interesting, "whether there be knowledge, it shall vanish away. For we know in part". Most churches seem to be focusing on something that's temporary and will vanish away. In this life we can never have perfect doctrine yet we think that we can perfect the saints, helping them to fulfill their destiny to be conformed to the image of Jesus, through doctrines that will vanish away. When we die our doctrines, imperfect because of our limitations, will become perfect. Paul confesses "now I know in part; but then shall I know even as also I am known". Only God can do this, when He reveals Himself to us, and we see Him as He truly is.

There is something we can and should do. Paul continues to say, " Now abideth faith, hope, charity, these three; but the greatest of these is charity." There are things that need to be developed in our lives if we are going to fulfill our destiny. Our character will not be automatically changed when we die. After we die there will certainly come a judgment. We will have to give an account of what we have done with the great salvation God has given us. The faith, the hope and the love that is perfected in us here and now will abide forever. I believe God wants to use His Church to perfect the saints, perfecting them in love. If our doctrines help us to grow in faith or hope or love, they are good doctrines. These doctrines may be different for different people. Because our knowledge is limited, these doctrines may pass away, but the faith, hope and love, that they produce, will last forever.

Far too many of our doctrines bring division and strife to the Body of Christ. Paul says in 1st Corinthians 1:10-12 "Now I beseech you, brethren, by the name of our Lord Jesus Christ, … that there be no divisions among you; … For it hath been declared unto me … that there are contentions among you. Now this I say, that every one of you saith, I am of Paul; and I of Apollos; and I of Cephas; and I of Christ." Paul's writing sounds like it could have been for us today. Paul, Apollos and

Peter were, all three, great teachers and good people. Today we have many churches that have great teachers, who are also good people. We also have some who only claim Christ as their founder. They also have some great teachers and good people. Wouldn't it be nice if we could love one another as Christians and embrace the things we have in common. We all need to increase in faith, hope and love. We are all walking toward our destiny. We will all be better off if we lift each other up instead of tearing one another apart. Jesus has suffered enough for us all. We don't need to make Him suffer more by cutting up His Body here on earth.

In John 17, just before He died, Jesus prayed, "Neither pray I for these alone, but for them also which shall believe on me through their word; that they all may be one; as thou, Father, art in me, and I in thee, that they also may be one in us: that the world may believe that thou hast sent me." We are the only ones who can answer this prayer. Jesus answers our prayers because of His love and mercy towards us. Shouldn't we answer His? While we stand divided the world remains in unbelief. What would happen if we could unite?

Chapter 4

Three Blind Mice

Three blind mice; see how they run. Let's call these three blind mice; the doctrines of the Nicolaitanes, the Gnostics, and the Judaizers. The Nicolaitanes had a doctrine that God hates. Revelations 2: 15 says, "So hast thou also them that hold the doctrine of the Nicolaitanes, which thing I hate." This doctrine seems to be one of the devil's best kept secrets. On the one hand some people believe it to be teaching that sin is totally unimportant because Jesus paid the penalty for it and therefore we are free to sin as much as we want. I suppose that might qualify as something God would hate, but hate is a very strong word. This also would be somewhat redundant because in the previous verse the doctrine of Balaam is condemned and we know that he taught Balac to lead Israel into sin. On the other hand there are those who point to the Greek meaning of the word. The first part of the word means conquest as in Nicopolis. The second part means over the people. It follows that this could mean the setting up of a hierarchy in the Body of Christ. This view makes it difficult to understand how the early Church justified elders, pastors, bishops and apostles, all of which seem to form a hierarchy. I don't believe the formation of a hierarchy is what God hates. I believe it is more likely the doctrines that some members of this hierarchy teach. Jesus doesn't hate the people. He said "which thing I hate." There can be a tendency within these hierarchies in the church for people to go too far, and become intermediaries between God and the people He loves. Just imagine for a moment that you want a romantic evening with your spouse and somebody butts in and says, "Wait a minute you need to go through me." I think you would probably hate that. I don't think hate is too strong a word for what God feels when somebody places himself between God and the people He loves. God's desire is to have direct fellowship with each one of us. It's very easy for people in leadership positions in the Church to teach, by either words or actions, that they are, mediators, providing access to God. When we, intentionally or unintentionally, assume this position, we injure people's ability to have a relationship with God and one another. It's only when we each have an individual relationship with God that we can be united in Him. God loves us and is jealous in a good way. He hates it when anything comes between Him and (you) the one He loves.

The second "mouse" is called Gnostic. These people have been around for a long time and apparently came into the Church with early Greek converts to Christianity. They were an exclusive club made up of people who had "special knowledge". They taught that the physical world and all material things were evil and spiritual things were good. An important aspect of this is that any sin that we would do now makes no difference because we will become spiritual beings, and as such, become good. This is an oversimplification of Gnosticism, but because much of what Gnosticism teaches varies from group to group and is not widely taught, I am not going to go into detail in this book. Instead, it is my desire to point out the most prevalent and destructive aspects. Believing that we have either exclusive or superior knowledge separates us from other Christians and therefore divides the Body of Christ. It should be obvious that this is prevalent in the modern Church and is part of the reason Christianity is so divided.

The belief that material things are evil and spiritual good is most commonly manifested in the modern Church in clever disguises. We believe we have to sin because we have a physical body or when we die our character will change because we leave this old flesh behind. The problem here is that we are making excuses for sin. This is the same thing that Adam and Eve did. We need to own up to our sins and confess them to God. We have no excuse. God has given us everything we need to overcome sin in our lives. Excuses always make sin seem less evil. When we excuse sin it becomes easier and we don't feel as badly about it. Sin will always destroy us, our fellowship with one another and our relationship with God. Excuses may make us feel better but what we need is forgiveness. "If we confess our sins, He is faithful and just to forgive."

The third mouse is "the Judaizers." Though Judaizers are most often thought of as people who want to bring us back to the Jewish Law, as a works-centered salvation, it creeps into our lives continually. It seems the longer we are in Church the harder it is to escape the belief that what we are doing is making us better than others. Saturday Night Live's "Church Lady" might serve as a great lesson. Sadly, there are many reasons that the world views us this way. I pray that I will never be one of those reasons. We wind up with our own language, a language that the world doesn't understand. Anytime we add works of any kind to salvation, we make the gap between God and the people He loves greater. We hinder the work of God by making it appear harder for people to be saved. The term "a baker's dozen" (13 instead of 12) comes from a habit of adding one so that we will never be guilty of short-changing someone by accidentally miscounting. This has been a Jewish tradition and, on the surface, seems very good. I for one certainly like the extra bagel. The problem with this thinking occurs because, when we start making rules that go beyond what God requires of us, we separate ourselves above others.

The one thing that all of these mice have in common is they separate us from one another and/or God. "They all run after the farmer's wife." These doctrines have plagued the Church from the beginning. Our enemy, the devil, cannot destroy the Church. Jesus promised us that the gates of hell would not prevail against us. The devil's tactic is to divide the Church. Just as division weakens a country, it also weakens the Body of Christ. The more distance the devil can put between God and those who do not yet believe in Jesus, the easier it is for him to bring them to hell. I have just hit some things here that are heavy on my heart. Much more could be said about the many things the devil and we ourselves are doing or believing to cause division. God's desire is for unity. Not a unity that accepts evil, but a unity that embraces the love, the joy, and the peace, the Kingdom of

God brings. Pride, envying, and arguing are tools the devil is using to try to destroy that Kingdom. When Jesus prayed for us to be united, the reason He gave was this, "that they may be made perfect in one; and that the world may know that thou hast sent me, and hast loved them, as thou hast loved me." It seems to me that surrendering our prideful independence is a small price to pay for so great a reward. We need each other far more than we realize. A divided Church can neither fulfill its obligation to perfect the saints nor can it fulfill its commission to reach the lost.

"She cut off their tails with a carving knife". We have a carving knife. It is called the "Sword of the Spirit". Many times good people carry these divisive doctrines. The Word of God is a useful tool to destroy these doctrines. Too often we try to kill the people with this sword or divide the Church. What we really need to do, is cut off the tail. Destroy divisive doctrines with the Word of God and prayer. Please pray with Jesus to unite the Body of Christ. Can you imagine what might happen if we all began to pray in agreement with Jesus that we might be one? "Have you ever seen such a sight in your life" as three blind, tailless mice and the Church united in Christ?

Chapter 5

Who said That?

In the third chapter of first Samuel, we have an interesting story about Samuel, as a child, and Eli. Samuel's mother had brought him to Eli shortly after he was weaned. Eli, at this time, was an old man with failing eyesight. He was both High Priest and Judge in Israel and Samuel was there to serve God and help Eli. One night Samuel heard a voice call out his name. He immediately ran to Eli, thinking it was him. This happened three times and the third time Eli realized God was speaking to Samuel. He told Samuel to go back to bed and, if it happened again, say, "speak, Lord; for Thy servant heareth."

As Christians, hearing and recognizing God's voice is extremely important. In the tenth chapter of John, Jesus gives us the example of a good shepherd caring for his sheep. He tells us that sheep both hear and recognize their shepherd's voice. Each sheep, we are told, is called by their own name. We cannot count on someone else to hear God's voice for us. In order to have the relationship with God that He wants for us, we must learn to hear and recognize His voice. John

10:16 says, "And other sheep I have, which are not of this fold: them also I must bring, and they shall hear my voice; and there shall be one fold, and one shepherd." In this passage, Jesus is addressing the Jewish Nation. Paul makes it clear to us that there is no difference between Jew and Gentile and no place for sectarianism in the Body of Christ. It is also apparent from the Book of Acts that salvation was not brought to the Gentile nations until after Jesus had ascended into heaven. Everyone who hears Jesus' voice after He ascended into heaven is hearing it in a different way than the Jews did when Jesus gave this teaching. Like Samuel, we might not even know when God is speaking to us. We might think that we are hearing our own thoughts. It's easy to think that being there with Jesus would make it so much easier to hear and recognize His voice. I wonder what Jesus was feeling when He said, "He that hath ears, let him hear." He said that many times. When I was younger I used to think He might be saying this to seal the fate of the Pharisees and scoffers. Now I wonder if it wasn't a deep felt prayer for those who were unable to recognize the voice of God. However or whenever Jesus speaks to us, there are always those who fail to hear and recognize His voice.

Romans 10:17 says, "So then faith cometh by hearing, and hearing by the word of God. But I say, Have they not heard? Yes." As Christians, each of us has heard God. The saving faith that God gives each one of us comes by hearing and we could not hear anything if God did not speak. Many of us may not even have realized that God was speaking to us, but He was. Oftentimes this is the way God speaks to us. He bypasses our minds and goes directly to our hearts. When Jesus places things in our hearts, we are given a choice whether or not to follow our hearts. Sometimes I have followed my heart and sometimes I haven't. I always regret the times when I don't do what God places in my heart.

God also speaks to our minds. When God is speaking to us in this way, we can sometimes hear an inner voice. I've heard this referred to as a "still small voice." Personally, I have found that the volume varies. At times there is indeed a still small voice, but other times it seems more like a regular conversation. A few times I've heard it loud enough to get my attention. God can also speak in an audible voice. We have Biblical accounts of God speaking from heaven at Jesus' baptism and Paul's conversion on the road to Damascus. When God speaks this way, there are times some people seem to hear him while others may not. Still other people only hear something that sounds like thunder. I don't pretend to fully understand this but I mention it because it points out the difficulty in determining whether God is speaking to our minds or audibly from heaven, especially, if it's loud enough to get our attention.

God can speak to us any time He wants. I believe He wants to speak to us most of the time but has to wait for a time when we will listen. When we are praying or reading the Bible we are usually in a more receptive state of mind. I think this is why most people believe they hear from God at these times. Paul was on his way to Damascus, planning the extermination of Christianity, when God spoke to him. For some unknown reason, that was the exact right time Paul was ready to receive it. God will speak to us to build us up one step at a time, giving us only what we are able to receive at a particular time in our lives. This is why we must always be moving toward our destiny. If we quit responding to what God tells us, He has no reason to tell us anything more. There have been times my Christian life has been stalled for that very reason.

Hearing is only one-third of the issue. The second part is recognizing His voice. I need to know if the inner voice speaking to my heart is God speaking to me, my own desire or anything else. No matter how or when God speaks to us His voice will always carry some very distinguishing characteristics. The first thing that distinguishes God's voice from anything else is the harmony it bears to His written word. God never contradicts Himself. His heart is always to bring us closer to Him and to each other. In our prayer life we should ask God to reveal His character to us. When God speaks He does not contradict His character. Early in my Christian walk I discovered mercy as an aspect of God's character. I was convinced forever that God's mercy is everlasting. From then on I knew that His voice would never contradict mercy. Because we are prone to misunderstand God's written word, from time to time, God's character can be a more reliable feature of His voice. Things like His goodness, love, holiness and mercy are absolute and unmistakable characteristics of His voice. The more we are convinced of and know God's character traits the better we can discern His voice. I hear my own voice quite often. I think my thoughts are wonderful thoughts. I'm always in full agreement with them. An important aspect of God's voice is that it's not like mine. God can take things that I hold sacred and dear and shatter them with a simple phrase. Jesus changed the whole world when He spoke two words, "Our Father". The ramifications of those two words changed the whole world forever. When God speaks to me I am usually totally blown away by what He says.

One day, when I was a young Christian involved in street evangelism, I found myself praying in our living room. I was standing in the middle of the floor, as I recall, and I was praying fervently to God. I wanted an anointing to bring the Gospel to the world. I never before had a two-way conversation with God. My prayers were all one way. I was asking for a good thing. I was asking for a good reason. I had my posture just right. I was certain I was in the center of God's will. All of a sudden a voice caught my attention. I'm not sure if it was one of those audible voices from heaven. It's hard to tell when an inner voice is that loud. The voice said, "How much anointing do you want?" I could barely believe it. I knew that wasn't my voice. I thought to myself "I have gotten **His** attention." What an opportunity! Boldly I told Him I wanted all the anointing I could get. He asked me, in a kind and loving voice that already knew the answer, "Do you want as much as Stephen?" How do I know that was God's voice? It's a quick and powerful sword that cuts away all my phoniness, pride and hypocrisy. It pierces to the heart and lays bare the soul. There is no easy set of rules we can set down for recognizing His voice. All we can do is let Him own us. We are, after all, **His** sheep, and the more we become **His** sheep the better we will recognize **His** voice.

This brings us to the third part. What do we do when we hear and recognize His voice? In the account I just gave you, my answer was "No". God had given me a wonderful opportunity and I turned it down. I wish I could say that each time I heard and recognized God's voice I responded by completely agreeing with Him, but I can't. The hard part is the failures. Even now, some thirty years later, my heart grows heavy when I recall that day. I have all I can do to contain my composure. I know His mercy endures forever. I know He loves me beyond measure. I know He died for me. I know He will lift me up. I know He forgives me completely. I know that I'm the only one who remembers this because He will not. I know my Savior lives and makes intercession for me even while I'm failing. I know He does the same for you. We are His favorite ones. Don't think for a minute that it doesn't make any difference whether I say yes or no. It's of the gravest importance that we always say yes. I pray for God's strength to help us always say yes. As we draw closer to God and understand His heart more, we begin to love one another more and become one in Christ. This takes two-way communication with God for each one of us.

Chapter 6

Liar, Liar, Pants on Fire

"The fearful, and unbelieving, and the abominable, and murderers, and whoremongers, and sorcerers, and idolaters, and **all liars**, shall have their part in the lake which burneth with fire." This quote, from Revelation 21:8, puts liars in some interesting company. I may be making more out of this than I ought to, but liars are the only ones that have the word "all" next to them. In the sixth chapter of Proverbs, we find six things God hates. "These six things doth the Lord hate: yea, seven are an abomination unto him: a proud look, a lying tongue, and hands that shed innocent blood, An heart that deviseth wicked imaginations, feet that be swift in running to mischief, a false witness that speaketh lies, and he that soweth discord among brethren." God expands this out to seven things that are an abomination to Him so that he can include both a lying tongue and a false witness that speaks lies. I think God might be trying to tell us something. Of the six things God hates, lies are hated twice. It can be truly said that God hates lying more than anything else on this list.

This is very disturbing to me. James tells us that our tongue is our most unruly member. Lying seems to be part of our very nature. We learn to lie at a very young age. There's a desire built into each of us to be loved and admired by others. I'm sure if my wife had seen me like I really am before we got married she would have never said, "I do." We call it putting our best foot forward, but it's really hiding our true selves. The world seems to see hypocrisy as our most prominent attribute. Wearing a mask becomes so natural we don't even realize we're doing it. These lies we tell other people are easily detected. It's still very difficult to overcome this type of lying but knowing that we are doing it is a great help.

When I lie to myself, I don't even know it. Even worse, I believe it. These lies are far more difficult to overcome. If I believe my own lies, I begin to do things that can lead to my own destruction. As an example, I might convince myself that I am a better driver than I really am and therefore able to exceed speed limits. I don't think that will end well. When I was praying in the last chapter, I had convinced myself that I wanted a great anointing. As a result, I told that same lie to God. Thank God He showed me what a fool I had been. In order to overcome being a liar, I need a lie detector.

For many years I was an electrical inspector. One day I was in an office building doing an electrical inspection. In new construction tape is usually placed on glass when it's installed so that it's visible and nobody walks into it. I saw a clear path between two offices and decided to take the shortcut. I walked, at a rather fast pace, into a glass partition. There was no tape on it. It was invisible. I hit that partition face first. I was in quite a bit of pain and wondering whether or not I had broken my nose. Suddenly an inner voice, loud enough to get my attention, said, "You always act on what you believe." Now that's the last thing I was thinking of, but it's what I needed to know. God gave me a lie detector. When I look at what I do, I become aware of what I really believe. Sometimes I'm very disappointed in myself. I have found that being honest with myself shows me how little faith I have and things I only think I believe in. Knowing these things, painful though it may be, is the first step in overcoming them. This is what James was talking about when he said, "faith without works is dead." This lie detector will only work to the degree we believe it will. We will never grow much spiritually until we can be honest with each other, ourselves and with God. God sees us as we really are and loves us beyond measure.

We can never fulfill our destiny until we can see ourselves as we really are, allow others to truly see us and still love one another.

Chapter 7

I Fought the Lord and the Lord Won

I've always loved a good Bible study. Even when I was a young boy in Catholic school, I did well in religious study (catechism). Sometimes that was all I was good at. Since I've been born again, I've attended Bible studies whenever I could. I studied on my own at home. I have a Strong's and a Young's concordance. I want to stay young and strong in my faith. I have an expository dictionary, topical bible, translations galore and even an interlinear Greek-English New Testament. I've gone through the Bible with J. Vernon McGee. As I said earlier I prayed "the sinner's prayer" at a Bible study. Did I mention? I've always loved Bible studies.

It was just an ordinary day. It was so ordinary; I don't even remember exactly what I was doing. I do remember that my wife was sitting at the computer and I was walking past her. An inner voice said, "Look up study". I was surprised because in all my study of the Bible I had never studied "study". It just never occurred to me. I knew that we are supposed to study the Bible diligently. It's the two main things we do as

Christians, pray and study the Bible. I thought to myself, "This is going to be a real waste of time." I also realized that "look up study" wasn't my own thought. I wouldn't have come up with this idea in a million years. I was pretty sure the devil wouldn't want me to look up anything in the Bible. By process of elimination I figured it must be God telling me to do this. I went upstairs and got my Strong's concordance and a Bible. I looked up the word "study." I was looking for a large column of references for the word and couldn't find it. I looked up study in the dictionary to make sure I was spelling the word right. My spelling is atrocious, but I was spelling it correctly. I went back to my Strong's and found what I was looking for. The word "study" occurs twice in the New Testament and once in the Old Testament. The word "studieth" occurs twice in Proverbs. Proverbs 15:28 says, "The heart of the righteous studieth to answer:" Proverbs 24:2 states, "For their heart studieth destruction, and their lips talk of mischief." In these two instances the likely meaning of study is to ponder a subject before you give an answer or to plan out a strategy. In the New Testament the word "study" is found in first Thessalonians 4:11 "that ye study to be quiet, and to do your own business." A paraphrase of this might be "work hard at being quiet and mind your own business." Second Timothy 2:15 says, "Study to shew thyself approved unto God, a workman that needeth not to be ashamed, rightly dividing the word of truth." The word "study" in this verse comes from the Greek root word spoude, pronounced spoo-day, which translates to speed. It has a sense of rushing forward with diligence to show ourselves approved unto God.

The only other place we see the word "study" is in Ecclesiastes 12:12 "And further, by these, my son, be admonished: of making many books there is no end; and much study is a weariness of the flesh." In this case the word "study" means study. At this point I was at least as upset about this as you probably are. I couldn't believe that "much study" is a weariness of the flesh. I began to argue with God. It was, after all, God who told me to look up "study" in the first place. I said, "Wait a minute, the Bereans studied, didn't they?" He said, "No they didn't." I replied "What do you mean?" He told me that they merely verified the revelation they had gotten from Paul. I was thinking to myself "This is crazy". I said, "We're supposed to meditate in the Word. I know the Bible says that." He said, "That's right." I was becoming frustrated. I told Him that I thought meditation and study were about the same thing. He said, "No they're not." I then said, "What's the difference?" He told me, "When you study you come to the word thinking you can figure it out. When you meditate you come to me, knowing you can't."

I'm pretty sure some people reading this will have a different understanding of these five verses than I present here. These differences of opinion are mostly caused by our differences of perspective. Most scholars realize that our personal prejudices and histories affect our perspectives on Bible passages. For this reason many have come up with rules that govern how we should interpret the Bible. Needless to say we can even find disagreement over these rules. The point I'm trying to make here might be better made if you think my assessment of these verses is wrong. What God is doing to change my life is far more important than my ability to understand these verses. If we are looking to doctrines to give us the truth, we are destined to fail. The truth is Jesus. That's why the truth can only be found in deepening our relationship with Him.

Because I believe God led me to this word study, I have given it much prayer, thought, and meditation. This is an account of something God is doing in my life. It is obvious that God directed me to study. A thorough knowledge of the Bible is a great asset. We cannot meditate on God's word if we don't know it. Even though I'm not sure that I'm correct in my understanding of these five scriptures, I am certain of what God told me. For me going to the Word and thinking I can figure it out is a prideful exercise in the flesh. Since that day, through prayer and meditation, my understanding of those verses has increased. What my study couldn't do, God is accomplishing by applying these verses to my heart. My study gained me some knowledge of the subject. Prayer and meditation have given me greater knowledge of the subject and built a greater relationship with God.

"Much study is a weariness of the flesh." Notice the word "much". God doesn't tell us not to study or that all study is bad. He is warning us of the possibility that some study can be an exercise in the flesh that causes us to strive about words to no profit and leads to mere vain babbling. Pride becomes a factor when we're the ones who have it all figured out. This type of study has divided the Body of Christ again and again. Meditation draws us closer to God. When we draw closer to God, we draw closer to each other.

God is not a science project. We need a relationship with Him not just knowledge about Him. Sometimes people will stalk other people. They will follow them around and learn all they can about them. This is not the kind of relationship we need. God desires, and we need, an intimate relationship. We cannot begin to fulfill our destiny until we know the very heart and mind of God. We are destined to be transformed by the renewing of our minds.

Our most intimate thoughts are poured out in our prayers. I believe it is the same for Jesus. He has shared some of His prayers with us. We have talked a little about Jesus' prayer in the 17th chapter of John. I believe it gives us great insight into Jesus' heart. The greatest emphasis in that prayer is for unity in the Body of Christ and that unity comes through our unity with Jesus and our Father. We may not agree on all of our doctrines but we can agree with Jesus and make the prayer of our heart His prayer for unity. I'm asking everyone, who calls upon the name of the Lord, to pray daily, in agreement with Jesus, for unity in the Body of Christ. I hope this will have two effects. The first is, we'll start answering Jesus' prayer by uniting in prayer with Him. The second great thing that will happen is, "that the world may believe that thou hast sent me."..."and hast loved them, as thou hast loved me."

Chapter 8

The Our Has Come

Two words changed the world forever. They are perhaps the greatest words that Jesus spoke. Until that day, when Jesus spoke those words, mankind's access to God was severely limited. Our understanding of God was seriously flawed. Our relationship with God was severely handicapped. Those two words were "Our Father". The moment Jesus said "Our" He changed my life completely. He declared His relationship with me. When I accepted that relationship, I began a new life in Him. John 1:12 puts it this way, "But as many as received Him, to them gave He power to become the sons of God." When Jesus said, "Our", He included all who receive Him. He also included all who believe on His name, those who are born of God. It doesn't stop there. That relationship is offered freely to everyone. This is the "Our" that has come. This is the "Our" that changed the world forever. The authority that we have to act in Jesus' name comes from this word, "Our". Jesus, with this one word, has partnered with us. Colossians 3:17 reveals His desire for us, "whatsoever ye do in word or deed, do all in the name of the Lord Jesus." Jesus wants that partnership to permeate every aspect of our lives and especially our prayer lives. This same word is an invitation to come alongside Jesus in intimate prayer. Jesus invites us to share His access to Our Father. We no longer need to seek God on our own. Jesus, who is the only begotten Son of God, has put a word in for us with His Father. It's as though we received a letter of introduction:

> Dearest Father,
>
> I would like to introduce my beloved brother. Please listen to his prayers. He is praying with me and the prayers I've put into his heart are my prayers also. Please treat him just as You would treat Me.
>
> Your loving and obedient Son,
>
> Jesus

Sadly, many people refuse this invitation. They either refuse to seek God at all or continue to seek God on their own.

Just as Jesus saying "Our" had ramifications that changed the world; there are great implications for our lives when we accept His invitation by saying "Our". Like the thief on the cross next to Jesus, we recognize that we need Jesus' help. We acknowledge that Jesus is heir to the throne, the Son of God. We accept the intercession Jesus makes for us. We identify with His death and resurrection when we reject our old ways and accept Jesus as our only way. I'm sure I don't fully understand all of the implications. I know that Jesus does and that's what really matters. It's no longer what I know. It's no longer my faith. It's no longer my righteousness. It's no longer anything of me. It's "Our......".

We have a choice. Who do we want to include when we say "Our"? I certainly want to include my wife and children. We can include our friends and neighbors. We can include people who have asked us to pray for them. There really is no limit to who we can include. Jesus included everyone. While we were yet sinners Jesus included us. We were all, indeed, enemies of Christ when He included us. Will we include our enemies? Will we pray for those who hate us? It's up to each of us to decide. Who will we include when we say "Our"?

In the Old Testament, God has many titles. Father, is not one of them. When Jesus revealed God as Our Father, both our understanding and our relationship with God were drastically changed forever. This concept of God was considered blasphemy by the religious leaders in Israel. Islam teaches that allah cannot have children. Without this revelation, of God as our Father, we can only be servants or slaves.

God has not changed but our understanding of God has changed dramatically. Adam was created in the image of God. God was, indeed, his Father. Sin separated Adam and all of creation from God. Until Jesus revealed God as Our Father, everyone that lived viewed God from this fallen world. Today, many people still have this veil over their face; "but their minds were blinded: for until this day remaineth the same veil untaken away in the reading of the old testament; which veil is done away in Christ." (2 Cor. 3:14) When we agree with Jesus, believing God is Our Father, that veil is taken away. We view God from a whole new perspective.

One day, while I was perusing scripture, a certain verse jumped out at me. Galatians 4:6 reads, "And because ye are sons, God hath sent forth the Spirit of his Son into your hearts, crying, Abba, Father. " I felt as though The Spirit was screaming within my heart. It was as though I had put that Spirit of His Son in a prison within my heart and He was screaming to be released. I became aware of this foolish thing I had done. Instead of growing into the son that God wanted me to be, I locked the Spirit of His Son up in my heart and became a servant instead. That Spirit was screaming, crying and pleading to be released. I realized that instead of praying "Our Father", I was praying "Lord, Lord". I had been a child far too long. Galatians 4:1 explains, "the heir, as long as he is a child, differeth nothing from a servant, though he be lord of all." The fact that I was praying Lord, Lord showed that I didn't really believe I was a son. As God began to change my heart, I became more the son I'm supposed to be and my prayers automatically became less, Lord, Lord, and more, "Our Father". When God's only begotten Son said, "Our Father" He showed us that God has given us the power to become His children. "But as many as received him, to them gave he power to become the sons of God, even to them that believe on his name." Indeed, we are children of God. When we are young Christians our perspective may be very similar to that of a servant. As we mature, our perspective continues to change.

Servants are subjects of the king and as such they come under the law. The king makes the rules. That's why they're known as rulers. The children of the king are heirs to the throne. They have a vested interest in seeing that the laws their father made are upheld. Servants have a completely different perspective of the law. Servants may view laws as inconvenient or obstacles to their happiness. They may think the laws are stupid. They probably live in fear of punishment they could receive for breaking these laws. I'm pretty sure when the king's children were young they probably had the same fear. Their father, the king, probably had a switch that fit his hand very well and conformed nicely to their rounder parts. By the time they reached adult-hood, they understood the motives that their father had for creating each law. They saw that the law brought good to the people and the kingdom. They understood the law as a stronghold against evil. While the servants may have seen the law as a curse, the princes saw it as their hope and promise.

Like anyone else, I fall short of being able to live a perfect and sinless life but I no longer view the commandments as commandments. I view them as promises. My perspective has changed. When I read "Thou shalt love the Lord thy God with all thy heart", I look forward to the day that promise will be fulfilled in my heart. While some view "Thou shalt" as "you must" I view it as a promise "You will". It's all a matter of perspective. If we are children, then we are children of the "promise" and no longer under the "law". God has started a work in us. He is well able to complete that work. He wants to complete that work. He will complete that work. The commandments are all promises of what we will be. Our destiny is to be conformed to the image of God. We are His children and He is our loving Father. It's only right that we should look like Him. When we see Him as He really is; we shall be like Him.

Chapter 9

Do We Have any Volunteers?

After "Our Father", Jesus said, "Who art in heaven". I suppose, if Jesus hadn't said that, we might think we are praying to our earthly fathers. Another obvious thought also arises. This could be the beginning of entering into worship. This thought tends to make sense because the next phrase is "hallowed be Thy name". The problem with this is; if we are entering into worship wouldn't it be better to worship Our Father as creator of heaven and earth? I think it's interesting that God created a place that He dwells in. If I think about this too long, my head hurts. To save us all from a bad headache, I'm going to make a point. God does not need a place to dwell. He created a place to dwell so that He could be separated from us. Hebrews 12:29 tells us "for our God is a consuming fire." If God dwelt on a mountain, everything that touched the mountain might die. If God dwelled in an ark, all who touched it might die. Just to look upon God from a cleft in a rock would have killed Moses. Because God loves us and is merciful, He protects us. God never desired to be separated from us. When our first parents accepted evil into their lives, the whole earth was cursed by their actions. One day this world will be consumed and a new world will be created. Until that time, God has created heaven as a place where He could be far enough away from us to keep us safe. Heaven is also a place where the redeemed from the earth can dwell with Him for a while. Revelation 21:1 says, "And I saw a new heaven and a new earth: for the first heaven and the first earth were passed away."

We have an interesting picture of heaven in the sixth chapter of Isaiah. Isaiah had a vision of God sitting on a throne in heaven with marvelous six-winged seraphim above Him. One seraph cried out to another in worship, "Holy, holy, holy, is the Lord of hosts: the whole earth is full of his glory." Heaven was shaken to its doorposts by the sound of His voice. The place was filled with smoke. I'm pretty sure Isaiah thought he was as good as dead. As we all know, where there's smoke, there's fire. Immediately Isaiah was aware of his sinful nature. He said, "Woe is me! for I am undone; because I am a man of unclean lips, and I dwell in the midst of a people of unclean lips." This is a picture of each of us before we become children of God. If nothing were done, we would all be consumed, at the very sight of God. One of the seraphim took a coal from off the altar and touched it to Isaiah's lips and said, "Lo, this hath touched thy lips; and thine iniquity is taken away, and thy sin purged." Jesus, from the altar of the cross, said, "Father forgive them." The flames from that altar descended from heaven and rested on the heads of 120 disciples in an upper room. That same "Holy" Spirit rests on each of us today who have accepted our great salvation. It is only our partnership with Jesus that allows us to enter into heaven and approach the throne of God. Through Jesus our iniquity is taken away and our sin is purged. In Hebrews 4 we are told, "Seeing then that we have a great high priest, that is passed into the heavens, Jesus the Son of God... Let us therefore come boldly unto the throne of grace."

Jesus, not only paid the price for our sins and gave us access to the throne of God, He also revealed the Father to us. In the 14th chapter of John, Phillip asked Jesus to show them the Father. Jesus responded, "Have I been so long time with you, and yet hast thou not known me, Philip? he that hath seen me hath seen the Father; and how sayest thou then, Shew us the Father? Believest thou not that I am in the Father, and the Father in me? the words that I speak unto you I speak not of myself: but the Father that dwelleth in me, he doeth the works. Believe me that I am in the Father, and the

Father in me." Everything that Jesus said and did revealed the Father to us. If revealing the Father to us was that important to Jesus, it is only because it is extremely important to God, our Father.

In the Old Testament God used people to reveal Himself to the world. He sent His only begotten Son, Jesus, in His image, to reveal Himself. Isaiah heard God say, "Whom shall I send, and who will go for us?" He answered, "Here am I; send me." Our Father is in heaven and Jesus is with Him making intercession for us. They are asking the same question. "Whom shall I send, and who will go for us?" As we recognize that our Father is in heaven we must decide what our answer will be.

The next words that Jesus said were, "hallowed be thy name." John tells us in his first epistle, "For there are three that bear record in heaven, the Father, the Word, and the Holy Ghost: and these three are one." In the Old Testament God revealed Himself through several names. In the New Testament Jesus revealed God through three names. Jesus revealed Him as Our Father, as our Savior and as the Holy Ghost. Jesus told us that He came in His Father's name and the name Jesus means God is salvation. When we pray with Jesus, "hallowed be Thy name," we are made mindful of the "Holy" Spirit.

In times past, churches have split over teachings about the Holy Ghost. I think part of the confusion could be cleared up by referring to Him as, "The Spirit of Holiness". If we're not becoming holy as He is holy, we might wonder if we have His Holy Spirit. It was no accident that God put a chapter about love right in the middle of two chapters about the gifts of the Holy Spirit. If we understand the relationship between love and holiness, we can understand why holiness is of primary importance as a motivator in the gifts of the Holy Spirit. Without love, we would soon be calling down fire from heaven on one another, if we had the power to do so.

If we choose to accept our Father's mission, we must remember that He is our Father, our Savior and Holy. Like Jesus, we represent Him by everything we say and do. We have an awesome responsibility to uphold God's name. In order to have credibility, we must keep His name holy. If this seems impossible, remember He has given us His Holy Spirit to help us. If we have indeed received that Holy Spirit, fruit will be evidenced in our lives. Paul tells us in Galatians 5, "But the fruit of the Spirit is love, joy, peace, longsuffering, gentleness, goodness, faith, meekness, temperance: against such there is no law." John tells us in the second chapter of his first epistle, "My little children, these things write I unto you, that ye sin not. And if any man sin, we have an advocate with the Father, Jesus Christ the righteous." John wrote this epistle to help us overcome sin in our lives. Some people would have us change the word "if" to "when". John allows, with that one word, the possibility of not continuing in sin. For us it is impossible. My hope rests in God, my Father, my Savior and the Spirit of Holiness. Like Paul, I cry, who shall deliver me? I thank God that Jesus ever lives to make intercession for me. I'm praying with Him, "hallowed be Thy name." I have confidence that God will hear and answer my prayer. We are predestined to be conformed to the image of His Son. We need to keep His name holy now so that we can bring the Gospel to a lost world with credibility giving honor to His name.

Chapter 10

It's No Picnic

Jesus continued to pray saying, "Thy kingdom come." John the Baptist had a very simple message. "Repent for the kingdom of God is at hand." If we were to cover everything that Jesus said about the kingdom of God, we would be writing another Gospel. After Jesus ascended into heaven, the apostles continued to speak of the kingdom of God. In the 20th chapter of Revelation we read, "They lived and reigned with Christ a thousand years." The Kingdom of God will be established on Earth for one thousand years. We look forward to this time when Jesus will rule and pray for its arrival. The saints of God have been looking forward to it for two thousand years and it still is a ways off. We will not enter into that reign until after the "great tribulation" period.

Many of the Jews, who had heard John the Baptist preach, believed that Jesus was going to set up His kingdom immediately. After seeing His miracles and being fed with only a few loaves and fishes, they hailed Him as King. This seems like a very logical reaction to what they had seen and heard. If the Kingdom of God is "at hand", we should expect that it wouldn't take two thousand years or more to arrive. Why would you preach to people who are only going to live seventy or eighty years, "The Kingdom of God is at hand", if they weren't going to live to see it? The answer lies in the 14th chapter of Romans. The 17th verse says, "The kingdom of God is not meat and drink; but righteousness, and peace, and joy in the Holy Ghost."

These three things are as available now as they were back then. In the sixth chapter of Matthew Jesus tells us to, "Seek ye first the kingdom of God, and his righteousness." He taught us to pray, "Thy Kingdom come."   The Kingdom of God must be prayed for and sought after diligently. It's no free lunch. If we are children of God and heirs to His Kingdom, our greatest desire should be to have His kingdom grow in our lives. Until God's Kingdom is strong in our lives, we will have difficulty bringing His Kingdom to others.

A while back God showed me that we are like conductors in an electrical circuit. God is using us to bring His Kingdom into the world. In order to do this well, we have to be good conductors. In electricity there are three things we can do to reduce the resistance of a conductor. There are also three things that will increase the Kingdom of God in our lives. These three things are faith, hope and love.   The big question is, "How can these three things be increased in our lives?"

In the seventeenth chapter of Luke, the Apostles asked Jesus to increase their faith. To this request Jesus replied,

> "If ye had faith as a grain of mustard seed, ye might say unto this sycamine tree, Be thou plucked up by the root, and be thou planted in the sea; and it should obey you. But which of you, having a servant ploughing or feeding cattle, will say unto him by and by, when he is come from the field, Go and sit down to meat? And will not rather say unto him, Make ready wherewith I may sup, and gird thyself, and serve me, till I have eaten and drunken; and afterward thou shalt eat and drink? Doth he thank that servant because he did the things that were commanded him? I trow not. So likewise ye, when ye shall have done all those things which are commanded you, say, We are unprofitable servants: we have done that which was our duty to do."

The key to increasing our faith is found in understanding the relationship between two words. The words are "faith" and "faithfulness". This relationship is found in the "lie detector" I mentioned earlier. Since we always act on what we believe, we prove our faith by what we do. James says it better when he tells us that "faith without works is dead." Dead things can't grow. We must first be faithful in little things before our faith can be increased into greater things. Faith is a gift from God. Faithfulness is our gift back to Him. Give and it shall be given unto you, pressed down and shaken together and running over.

When Paul told us that faith, hope and love would endure, he said, "The greatest of these is love." Once faith has germinated the seed of our salvation, it continues to grow. Hope and love are a result of this growth. Since God is love, the path to our destiny, to be conformed to His image, will follow this path. The first five verses in the fifth chapter of Romans spells this out for us.

> "Therefore being justified by faith, we have peace with God through our Lord Jesus Christ: by whom also we have access by faith into this grace wherein we stand, and rejoice in hope of the glory of God. And not

70

only so, but we glory in tribulations also: knowing that tribulation worketh patience; and patience, experience; and experience, hope: and hope maketh not ashamed; because the love of God is shed abroad in our hearts by the Holy Ghost which is given unto us."

Notice the progression here. God gives us faith to receive our salvation, bringing us peace. As our faith endures, we stand in His grace, waiting for our destiny to be fulfilled. This produces a great hope that God will complete the work that He has started in us. Along this path, we will find difficulties. From time to time we fail. We fall short. Trials and tribulations of all sort will be met along the way. If we patiently endure all these, trusting in God, we gain experience. These experiences cause our hope to soar. The more we see God move in our lives, the more extravagant our hope becomes. Eventually, we may even hope for all things. "Love.....hopeth all things." Oh! What joy shall fill my soul.

Just as faith brings us peace with God and hope brings us the joy of salvation in the midst of tribulation, love brings us righteousness. My "lie detector" has shown me, time and time again, I

don't love Jesus as I ought. Each time I sin, I prove
that I don't really love Jesus. Jesus told us, "If you
love me,you will keep my commandments." If I
truly loved Jesus, the outcome would be perfect
obedience. When I'm honest with myself, I find
myself beside Peter on the seashore talking to
Jesus. My sin betrays my lack of love for Jesus.
Jesus asks me if I love Him with all my heart. My
answer is, "I love you, but not that much." By the
third time, Jesus asks me if I love Him at all. He
sees my heart and knows that I'm not yet made
perfect in love. I want my love to grow. I see it
growing little by little, day by day. I want my love
to grow faster and stronger.

Luke 7:47 says, "Wherefore I say unto thee, Her
sins, which are many, are forgiven; for she loved
much: but to whom little is forgiven, the same
loveth little." There is an old, seldom-spoken of,
doctrine called, "the total depravity of man." One
day I looked deep into my heart and asked the Holy
Spirit to show me what was there. In my heart I
saw the roots of every evil known to mankind.
Until then, I didn't know how much forgiveness I
needed. I had so much sin I could never confess it
all. I had sin that I could not cease committing. I
had no escape. I was face to face with the "total
depravity" within me. Like Paul, I knew I was chief

among sinners. I cried out unto God and thanked Him that I am delivered through Jesus. My love for God, my Savior, grew a great deal that day. I cannot bypass my "lie detector". If I don't love others, who I see, how can I love God, who is invisible? When I realize my total depravity; my perspective changes with regard to everyone else. I can no longer look down on anyone. I am at the bottom looking up. God has given me faith to believe I have a destiny. My hope endures until that destiny will be fulfilled. That destiny can only be fulfilled when His love is perfected in me. When I love perfectly, all sin in my life will cease. Until then, twenty-four hours a day, seven days a week, I continue to break the first and greatest commandment. "Thou shall love the Lord thy God with all thy heart". For me, this is not a command, it's a promise. One day, that promise will be fulfilled and we will know the glory we have in Him. Let "Thy Kingdom come" into our hearts.

Chapter 11

Too Many Questions; Not Enough Answers

"Thy will be done", raises some questions. Is there anything that happens that isn't God's will? Are there things that happen in heaven that aren't God's will? Are there things that happen on earth that aren't God's will? "On earth as it is in heaven", adds more questions. We know more about hell than we do about heaven, and we know more about earth than we do about hell. It seems to me the thing we know least about is God's will. This is definitely an area where we have more questions than answers. We can sometimes make the mistake of focusing on things we cannot be certain of. Since we cannot always know the answers to our questions, there can be times we should focus more on our questions than our answers.

All things are created by God. Nobody forced Him to create anything. It seems obvious that He did it willingly. The argument goes on to say, because all things are created by the will of God, even evil and disasters must be part of God's will. When Jesus prays, "Thy will be done", He assumes that God's will is not always being done. When God finished creating the world He said, "It is very good". Shortly thereafter, Adam and Satan corrupted mankind and the world. Wherever the argument goes from there; makes no difference to me. Jesus' prayer tells me, not everything that happens is God's will. I will always take Jesus' side in prayer over any argument. First Peter 3:9 tells us, "The Lord is not slack concerning his promise, as some men count slackness; but is longsuffering to us-ward, not willing that any should perish, but that all should come to repentance." People perish every day and it's not God's will. People refuse to be born again every day and it's not God's will. God's will isn't always done on earth.

Another question arises. Is God's will always done in heaven? Was it God's will Satan decide to elevate himself above God? Was it God's will that the devil corrupt one-third of the angels? Is it God's will for the evil one to accuse Christians? Is it God's will to have war in heaven? I don't know all the answers. For some of these questions, I can only speculate what the answers might be. I am certain God's will, shall prevail eventually both in heaven and on earth. Meanwhile, God's will seems to be thwarted everywhere. For the time being, it can be difficult to know the will of God in either place.

Instead of trying to figure out the answer to these questions, I suggest we focus on questions we know some answers to. Some of these questions might be, "What has God revealed to us about His will in heaven?" "What changes, do we think, need to occur to bring about His will being done on earth as it is, in His revealed will, in heaven?" "Where do these differ?" If we are to pray with Jesus for God's will to be done, here and now, on earth as it is in heaven, we have to acknowledge the differences between His clearly revealed will in heaven and our perception of His will on earth.

Jesus came to reveal God's will to us. Everything that Jesus said and did reveals that will to us. The apostle John ends his gospel saying, "And there are also many other things which Jesus did, the which, if they should be written every one, I suppose that even the world itself could not contain the books that should be written." We could meditate on the things that Jesus did, revealing God's will, for the rest of our lives and never exhaust the subject. Luke tells us in the fourth chapter, "The Spirit of the Lord is upon me, because he hath anointed me to preach the gospel to the poor; he hath sent me to heal the brokenhearted, to preach deliverance to the captives, and recovering of sight to the blind, to set at liberty them that are bruised, to preach the acceptable year of the Lord. ….He began to say unto them, This day is this scripture fulfilled in your ears." Jesus turned water into wine, healed the sick, raised the dead, multiplied loaves and fishes, walked on water, calmed the storm, and all before He rose from the dead. Jesus told us that we would do the works that He did. I can make foolish excuses or admit that I have not done these works. Since Jesus brought salvation to everyone, I would be hard put to do greater works by preaching the Gospel to my generation. I have to be honest and admit my failures.

Jesus died on a cross for my sins. God's will for me is to give my life, a sacrifice, for others. My grade here is also an "F". Jesus was tested just as I am tested. He got an "A+". I got an "F". We are destined to be conformed to the image of Jesus. That's God's will for me. That's God's will for me in heaven. That's God's will for me on earth. Jesus is praying His prayer of intercession for us each day before the throne of God. He knows that I failed, each and every day, to do God's will. He will never give up on me. He will never give up on you. He will continue to intercede for us until that prayer is answered. Some people don't know that Jesus is praying this prayer for them every day. For a long time I didn't know it. This does not change the fact. Jesus will continue to pray for us every day, just because He loves us. It's God's will for Jesus to intercede for us daily in heaven. We know, Jesus taught us to pray, "Thy will be done on earth as it is in heaven." As long as we live we can make intercession for each other every day. We can agree on earth, in prayer, even if we don't know we're agreeing with Jesus in heaven. Hebrews 7:25 says, "Wherefore he is able also to save them to the uttermost that come unto God by him, seeing he ever liveth to make intercession for them." I believe that Jesus will be praying this prayer daily until it is ultimately answered. He is interceding for us, praying until we are saved to the uttermost, "conformed to His image."

The hosts of hell, who delight in dividing the body of Christ, do not want us to unite with Jesus in this prayer daily. They have spread fear and erroneous teaching to prevent it. I want to take a little time here to put those fears to rest. In the sixth chapter of Matthew Jesus teaches about prayer.

> "And when thou prayest, thou shalt not be as the hypocrites are: for they love to pray

standing in the synagogues and in the corners of the streets, that they may be seen of men. Verily I say unto you, They have their reward. But thou, when thou prayest, enter into thy closet, and when thou hast shut thy door, pray to thy Father which is in secret; and thy Father which seeth in secret shall reward thee openly. But when ye pray, use not vain repetitions, as the heathen do: for they think that they shall be heard for their much speaking. Be not ye therefore like unto them: for your Father knoweth what things ye have need of, before ye ask him."

The first thing Jesus is teaching here is we should not be hypocrites. He's not teaching us that public prayer is evil. Hypocrisy is evil. Prayer is good, wherever and whenever we do it. If we view this first part as if public prayer were bad, we should close down all the churches and hide in our closets and pray. That's ridiculous and certainly not what Jesus is teaching. We should not pray intending to impress others with our spirituality. Our intentions in prayer need to be as pure as we can make them. Public corporate prayer unites congregations. Jesus prayed for this unity out loud and in public. That prayer did not make Jesus like a hypocrite.

We all seem to understand this, in part anyway, because we still pray in church and sometimes in private.

The second thing Jesus is teaching is sincerity in prayer. Jesus is not teaching us that repeating a prayer verbatim is bad. From some teachings I've heard, I could believe the teachers never read Psalms. One-hundred and fifty prayers were written down for a reason. Do we think they were written down so that we could make a hundred paraphrases of them? We sing songs in church to worship God. Shall we have the worship leader change the words each time so we can have confusion? God is not the author of confusion! The songs we sing are prayers of worship. I was a worship leader for many years. I know from experience sometimes these songs, these prayers, are vain repetition. We can tell by the expressionless faces. That's what Jesus is talking about. If we don't believe it, if we don't feel it, and if we don't mean it, it's just vain repetition. Reciting the same words together in prayer unite us in agreement the same way singing a familiar song unites us in worship. Again, it's not the repetition that's bad; it's the vain hypocrisy that Jesus is teaching against. We have another account of Jesus teaching His disciples to pray yet a second time in His ministry. Luke chapter eleven gives an account that is slightly different from "Our Lord's Prayer" in Matthew. These two accounts appear to be two different occasions. The account in Luke seems to be the second occasion mentioning this prayer. In Luke's account Jesus tells His disciples, "When ye pray, say, "Our Father"." The two prayers are nearly identical and pray the same thoughts in the same order. Jesus also repeated prayer in the Garden of Gethsemane just before His crucifixion. Sweating drops like blood is a good indication that the repetition is not vain. Satan wants to keep the Body of Christ separated. Jesus wants us to unite. We may never agree on doctrine. We may have different administrations governing our assemblies. If the devil can keep us from agreeing with one another and Jesus in this prayer, that Jesus gave His disciples on two occasions, he has won a great victory. My heart longs for unity. Jesus longs for unity. What will we do?

Chapter 12

Power Up

Before I get to the really good stuff, I need to do a brief recap of what God has shown us in the last four chapters. In chapter 8, we became children of God and joint heirs to His Kingdom through Jesus. In chapter 9, we became aware of the mission God has for us to represent Him and bring honor to His Name. In chapter 10, we begin to allow the Kingdom of God to be formed in us, preparing us, to bring it to a lost world. In chapter 11, we received clarification of our mission plan. We begin to understand what God wants to be done on earth and we realize we have a totally impossible task set before us. If God doesn't make a way for us to do this, there is no way we can accomplish anything.

As soon as we realize we have an impossible task, Jesus teaches us to pray, "Give us day by day our daily bread." This version of Our Lord's Prayer comes from Luke chapter 11. In Matthew we have the first account of Jesus sharing His prayer with us. He gives us this prayer in the middle of the "Sermon on the Mount." He says, "After this manner therefore pray ye." It is given in the middle of a teaching on how to pray and how not to pray. It would be nice to see the manner in which Jesus prayed that prayer. Based on His teachings we can imagine. In Luke we have a totally different picture. Jesus had just finished praying. One of His disciples asked Him to teach them "to pray". In response to this Jesus said the following:

> "When ye pray, say, Our Father which art in heaven, Hallowed be thy name. Thy kingdom come. Thy will be done, as in heaven, so in earth. Give us day by day our daily bread. And forgive us our sins; for we also forgive every one that is indebted to us. And lead us not into temptation; but deliver us from evil."

Jesus then follows up with a parable about a man seeking bread in the middle of the night, admonitions to ask, seek, and knock unceasingly and an assurance that if we ask for bread we won't get a stone. In short, when the disciple asked Jesus to teach him to pray He said when you pray don't forget to say my prayer first. It only makes sense for us to join with Jesus in His prayer first, when we enter into Our Father's throne. It is, after all, only through Jesus that we have access to His Father's throne.

Up to this point, the prayers in Matthew and Luke are virtually identical. Here Jesus says, "day by day" and in Matthew He says, "Give us this day." This may seem to be of little significance. It's not. Jesus is emphasizing that this prayer needs to be said day by day; not just this day. Jesus would not ask us to say this prayer every day if He wasn't doing it Himself. In Hebrews the fourth chapter we read, "Seeing then that we have a great high priest, that is passed into the heavens, Jesus the Son of God, …. Let us therefore come boldly unto the throne of grace." Jesus, our High Priest, makes intercession for us. I believe His prayer is a prayer of intercession for us. Jesus will continue to pray and intercede for us until His prayers are answered and our destinies are fulfilled.

Because Jesus is teaching his disciples "to pray", He focuses on the portion, "Give us day by day our daily bread." Jesus gives us this parable as an explanation of this passage.

> "Which of you shall have a friend, and shall go unto him at midnight, and say unto him, Friend, lend me three loaves; for a friend of mine in his journey is come to me, and I have nothing to set before him? And he from within shall answer and say, Trouble

me not: the door is now shut, and my
children are with me in bed; I cannot rise
and give thee. I say unto you, Though he
will not rise and give him, because he is his
friend, yet because of his importunity he
will rise and give him as many as he
needeth."

In the first part of Our Lord's Prayer, we became
aware of two things; a needy world and our
inability to meet that need. In this parable we have
a picture of a needy friend on a journey and a
man's inability to give him bread. Just as the
person in the parable seeks bread from his
neighbor, we need to get bread from our heavenly
Father. We have nothing in ourselves to offer a
world in need. In the next two verses, "And I say
unto you, Ask, and it shall be given you; seek, and
ye shall find; knock, and it shall be opened unto
you. For every one that asketh receiveth; and he
that seeketh findeth; and to him that knocketh it
shall be opened", Jesus reveals to us that if we ask,
seek, and knock with perseverance we will receive,
find and open "our daily bread". In the next two
verses Jesus explains to us that we're not dealing
with our next door neighbor who requires nagging
to be jarred from his sleep. We are asking bread
from our Father in heaven who loves us far more

than any earthly father has ever loved his children. Finally, Jesus says, "How much more shall your heavenly Father give the Holy Spirit to them that ask him?" The continual asking, seeking and knocking is not to raise God out of His slumber; it is to prepare us to receive, find, and open the Holy Spirit in our lives.

The devil has stirred up much controversy over receiving the "Baptism of the Holy Spirit", causing division in the Body of Christ. Jesus wants unity in the Body of Christ and my heart also breaks for that unity. Jesus said, God would give the Holy Spirit to anyone who asks for it. If we need evidence that we have received the Holy Spirit, we need only look to His first name "Holy". To find the Holy Spirit, we must diligently seek the fruit of the Spirit, in our lives, on a daily basis. That love of God is spelled out for us in Galatians fifth chapter, "But the fruit of the Spirit is love, joy, peace, longsuffering, gentleness, goodness, faith, meekness, temperance: against such there is no law." This is what the holiness of the Holy Spirit produces in our lives.

In the twelfth chapter of first Corinthians Paul tells us, "But covet earnestly the best gifts." There are times God intervenes directly into the affairs of men. The gifts of the Holy Ghost are supernatural empowerments from God and as such they are classified as divine intervention. When this happens, we can be certain that God's will in heaven is being done on earth. When God performs a miracle, we are certain that miracle is according to His will. When the Holy Spirit prays through us, we are certain it's according to God's will. If we pray for somebody and they are healed, we know this healing was God's will.   The manifestation of the gifts of the Holy Ghost is God's will. The best gift, the one we must covet earnestly, is the one that is needed right now. The gift of tongues would be the most important gift if we didn't know how to pray for something. That same gift will not bring us healing. Healing will not bring us wisdom.

When we are praying daily for our daily bread, we are asking God to fill us anew with His Holy Spirit. Day by day we need to seek earnestly the fruit of that Holy Spirit in our lives. The more that fruit is perfected in our lives, the more prepared we will be to bring the good news to a needy world. We are asking our Father to supply us with the supernatural power that we need each and every day. Our daily bread is a "power bar". We must ask for the Holy Ghost, seek His fruit diligently, and covet earnestly His supernatural power each and every day, so that we can have hope. Jesus is praying for us. When we enter into His prayer, He's praying with us. Unity in the Body of Christ will only come when we first unite with Him. The devil will do all he can to keep us from praying with Jesus. He knows what power will be unleashed on earth when the Church unites in Christ. The fear of repeating Our Lord's Prayer, that is rampant in the Church, is paranoia spread by Satan himself to keep the Body of Christ divided. In Matthew Jesus taught us to pray from our hearts earnestly. In Luke He taught us to pray and say Our Lord's Prayer in union with Him day by day. Some will continue in fear. Others will come together in love. We all have a free will.

Chapter 13

A Hole We Can't Get Out Of

My understanding of Our Lord's Prayer has changed over the years. As I continue, daily, to meditate on this prayer, I am certain my understanding will continue to grow. This is Jesus' prayer, and as such, it is as multi-faceted as Jesus Himself. I don't believe eternity has enough time to fully explore the depths of this heartfelt prayer of Jesus. When I first began to realize that Jesus is praying this prayer, I was confused by the words, "forgive us our debts." I asked Jesus how He could pray it. Since Jesus is without sin, it made no sense to me. He told me that He took the sins of the world on Himself. When Jesus intercedes for us, He first owns our sin. He takes them on as if they were His own sins and asks His heavenly Father to forgive those sins just as He forgives everyone who sins against Him. Jesus places no conditions on His forgiveness. He prayed, from the cross, "Father forgive them for they know not what they do." This is unconditional forgiveness. This is total forgiveness. This forgiveness is available to everyone who has ever sinned. The statement, "for they know not what they do", is not a condition. It is a statement of fact.

In Luke's version of Our Lord's Prayer Jesus says, "And forgive us our sins; for we also forgive every one that is indebted to us." Our sins differ as much or more from the debts owed to us as the debts mentioned in Jesus' parable. People owe us nothing in comparison to the "everything" we owe God. Jesus is telling us to say, forgive us for our sins (which are grievous) because we forgive the (insignificant by comparison) debts that are owed to us.

In Matthew's account Jesus prays, "And forgive us our debts, as we forgive our debtors." Because Jesus is God manifest in the flesh, He uses the same word in both places. The debts we owe Jesus are equal to the debts we owe God. When Jesus teaches us to pray, we ask forgiveness because we forgive others. When Jesus intercedes for us and shows us how to pray, He uses the word "as". The word "as" here means at the same time, or in the same manner. As I stated earlier, Jesus places no conditions on His forgiveness of us. He's asking us to come alongside Him and pray with Him for forgiveness as "we" forgive others. The choice is ours.

Jesus has left room in both versions of His prayer for us to choose. In Luke, we can choose to forgive and be forgiven or not forgive. If we choose the latter, our prayer will be untrue. In Matthew, as a result of Jesus' partnership with us, we are able to place conditions on forgiveness. It's not just whether or not we forgive, it's what conditions do we place on that forgiveness. By choosing the conditions we place on forgiving others, we place the same conditions on God. If we choose to wait a while before we forgive, God will honor that and wait to forgive us. If we choose to wait for repentance, God will honor our choice and expect repentance from us. There's no end to the limits we can place on God. The question is, why would we put any limits on Him; especially when it comes to our forgiveness?

Jesus is perfectly clear on this issue. In the eighteenth chapter of Matthew, Peter asked Jesus how often he should forgive. Jesus tells him to forgive four hundred and ninety times a day. This is more than once every three minutes. He then tells a parable about a man who is forgiven a tremendous debt. In spite of the fact that he was forgiven this debt, he refuses to forgive a much smaller debt owed him by another person. In the short version, he throws his debtor into prison and gets thrown into prison himself by the man he owed the tremendous debt to. Jesus finishes with this statement, "And his lord was wroth, and delivered him to the tormentors, till he should pay all that was due unto him. So likewise shall my heavenly Father do also unto you, if ye from your hearts forgive not every one his brother their trespasses."

Jesus tells us in Matthew, right after He prayed, "For if ye forgive men their trespasses, your heavenly Father will also forgive you: but if ye forgive not men their trespasses, neither will your Father forgive your trespasses." In Matthew alone, Jesus has told us this in prayer, twice directly and in parable. Jesus explained it four times in three different ways to make it perfectly clear. We cannot bring the message of God's forgiveness in word only. People see right through it. The Body of Christ is ridiculed as a den of hypocrites. Unforgiveness is a horrible sin in itself. It destroys the work God is trying to do. It is the direct opposite of what Jesus accomplished on the cross. It also makes it impossible for God to forgive us.

Some of us have had terrible things done to us, unthinkable things, and even things we consider unforgiveable. Does this mean we will go to hell if we can't forgive someone? Does this mean unforgiveness is an unforgiveable sin? We feel trapped in a pit with no way out. At times like this, when faced with impossible contradictions, we begin to try and rationalize our way out. The temptation arises to deny the truth and believe something less. However we rationalize it, the problem will never be fixed until we face it head on.

When God showed me how desperately evil I am, I realized that I could not repent of all my sins. There is no way I could stop doing some of the things that were sin in my life. I could not confess all of the sin in my life. I knew I did not love God or my neighbor in the way God commands me. I was trapped in a pit with no way out. I live twenty-four hours a day, every minute and every second sinning against those two greatest commandments. If Jesus hadn't given me a ladder to get out of that pit, I could have died of despair. I could not rationalize my way around what God had shown me. If I denied my sin I would become a liar. John told us,

> "If we say that we have no sin, we deceive ourselves, and the truth is not in us. If we confess our sins, he is faithful and just to forgive us our sins, and to cleanse us from all unrighteousness. If we say that we have

not sinned, we make him a liar, and his
word is not in us."

Rationalizing our way around God's truths is
actually lying to ourselves. Instead of confessing
our sin we find ways to tell ourselves we have not
sinned. We make Him a liar. God can begin to
solve this problem when we confess our sin.
Honesty is always a good first step. We must be
honest with ourselves and with God. Confessing
my sin is the first step out of the pit. It is the first
rung of the ladder. Two things happened when I
confessed my sin. They didn't happen because I
confessed my sin. They happened because Jesus is
faithful even when I'm not. Jesus not only forgives
our sin, He cleanses us from "ALL
UNRIGHTEOUSNESS". We have a DESTINY. We are
destined to be conformed to the image of Jesus.
We are destined to be sons of God. Jesus has
claimed us as adopted brothers. We are children
of God. As children of God, our perspective of the
law is changed forever. Where others have
commandments, we have promises. God, who
began a work in us when we were born again, will
complete that work and fulfil our destinies. We
will love God with all our hearts and with all our
souls.   We will love one another as God has loved
us. We will forgive others as God has forgiven us.

With Jesus, all things are possible. As we draw closer to Jesus and agree with Him in prayer, His prayer is answered. The unconditional forgiveness He gives us becomes the unconditional forgiveness we give others. Not only is our unforgiveness forgiven, our unforgiveness is healed. There's no part of our Christian walk we can walk in our own power. Realizing the total impossibility of living a Christian life apart from Jesus gives us a true perspective. We must always rely on Jesus to make the impossible in our lives possible. Just as we cannot be born again without faith, we cannot make this journey without hope. This hope is the second rung on the ladder God has given us. Our hope is in God's ability to complete the work he started in us. Without Him we can do nothing. With Him we can do all things.

I need unconditional forgiveness for all my sins. Jesus offers it to me. The good news is this. Jesus has invited us to come alongside Him in prayer as He intercedes for us. When Jesus says this part of the prayer He places no conditions on it. All we need to do is draw closer to Him. When we pray this prayer with Jesus, our conditions begin to fade away in the glory of His unconditional love and forgiveness. As I pray with Jesus day by day I slowly build a closer relationship with Him. We become like those we spend the most time with. Husbands and wives who have been married for years become more and more like each other. The more time I spend with Jesus, sharing His most intimate thoughts in prayer, the more I become like Him. I will not wait for them to repent. I will not demand a confession. I will, through God's grace, forgive as I am forgiven. I will forgive instantly and unconditionally.

Chapter 14

Changing Our Want-tos

In the fourth chapter of Matthew we read, "Then was Jesus led up of the Spirit into the wilderness to be tempted of the devil." In both Matthew's and Luke's account of Our Lord's Prayer, we're told to pray, "And lead us not into temptation; but deliver us from evil." Only fourteen verses, in Matthew, separate His Sermon on the Mount from His temptation in the wilderness. Jesus could have been thinking "I sure don't want to go through that again." I'm pretty sure that's not what He's praying about. James says some interesting things that might help us understand.

> "My brethren, count it all joy when ye fall into divers temptations; knowing this, that the trying of your faith worketh patience. But let patience have her perfect work, that ye may be perfect and entire, wanting nothing.".... "Blessed is the man that endureth temptation: for when he is tried, he shall receive the crown of life, which the Lord hath promised to them that love him."

James also says,

> "Let no man say when he is tempted, I am tempted of God: for God cannot be tempted with evil, neither tempteth he any man: but every man is tempted, when he is drawn away of his own lust, and enticed. Then when lust hath conceived, it bringeth forth sin: and sin, when it is finished, bringeth forth death."

All of these words for temptation are closely related in Greek. It's obvious, from the context, we are talking about two different things.

The first thing we're talking about is the trials that come into our lives from the outside. This is the type of trial that Jesus endured in the wilderness. It's the type of trial that comes from the persecution of Christians. These trials will test our faith, proving whether or not it will endure. James tells us we should rejoice when these trials come upon us. I have a hard time doing that. I want to pray with Jesus, "lead us not into temptation." I should be rejoicing. God will lead us into this type of temptation so that we can learn patience. The trials, that God leads us into, are tools God is using to perfect us. Our faith must join with patience to produce hope in our lives. Without hope, many of us would drop out of the race. Without hope none of us can win. The prize set before us is the destiny God has for us. When I realize this, I no longer want to pray away these trials. I want to rejoice in the mercy of God, who loves me enough to complete His work in me. This is our first changed "want-to".

The second thing we're talking about is temptation that leads to sin. There is really only one reason I sin; well, maybe two. First I don't love Jesus. Jesus said, "If you love me, you will keep my commandments." The second is because I want to. This second reason proves the first. This is a place where my "lie detector" comes in handy. We have all heard teaching about temptation. God could not have made it any plainer than He did through James. "every man is tempted, when he is drawn away of his own lust, and enticed." These temptations come from within. When the devil tempts us, we usually don't even know it, but that's another subject altogether. Anytime our "want-to" has the opportunity, it does whatever it wants and that leads to death (separation from God).

The typical teaching on temptation goes something like this.

> We are all tempted from time to time. It's not bad to be tempted. It's only bad if you succumb to the temptation. "You can't stop a bird from landing on your head but you can keep him from building a nest there."

This teaching starts out fine. We **are** all tempted from time to time. Jesus tells us to pray that we not be led into temptation. Before we rationalize this statement, let's get another one to rationalize. Jesus said, "whosoever looketh on a woman to lust after her hath committed adultery with her already in his heart." We can kid ourselves with rationalizations or agree with Jesus. As soon as my "want-to" clicks in I'm already guilty in my heart. Until we admit the truth, our prayer, "lead us not into temptation", is a sham.

Once we admit we have a problem, we are well on the way to victory. God wants to lead us into the truth that will set us free and change our "want-tos". God wants to deliver us from the evil desires in our hearts. He wants to deliver us from the "evil one" who desires our destruction. God tells us in Romans 12, to be "transformed by the renewing of your mind, that ye may prove what is that good, and acceptable, and perfect, will of God." If we are to prove to the world God's perfect will, we must have our "want-tos" changed. Our way of thinking must be renewed. Truth is not something we know. It is not a set of doctrines. Jesus is the truth. We must put on the mind of Christ. When we talk about sin in soft gentle terms, we miss the mark. Sin in any measure is horrendous. I could fill a library with adjectives depicting the vileness of sin and not come up to a fraction of its measure. This only begins to describe the smallest sin. When we pray with Jesus, we are asking our Father to lead us to that place where we will see sin as it really is. When I look at temptation in my own life, I see a place where the light of God's truth has not removed my desire to sin from my heart. The fact that I am tempted shows me I still don't love God with all my heart. His work is not complete in me. I can say "I want to be like Jesus" but my temptations tell me different. I am only tempted to evil because evil still resides in my heart. I know my redeemer lives. He makes intercession for us daily. As I join with Him in prayer, I have faith our prayers will be answered. This hope endures. My "want-tos" change.

The evil one (Satan) desires to destroy us physically and spiritually. If he can't do that, he will try to make us ineffective. His greatest tool has always been half-truths. Our greatest defense is truth itself. In John 17:17 Jesus prays, "Sanctify them through thy truth: thy word is truth."...." that they also might be sanctified through the truth." Just as half-truths imprison us, the truth sets us free. We are set apart (sanctified) and made holy by knowing the truth. As we have seen, the truth can sometimes be painfully disturbing. When we study God's word, we view it through many lenses. Each of these lenses distorts the truth. When we meditate in God's word, we view it through the eyes of the author. Seeing sin as God sees it, will sanctify us. Satan wants us to miss the mark and see sin as inconsequential. Jesus' sacrifice has delivered us, by grace, from the consequences of sin. The less we count the consequence of sin, the less we value the sacrifice of Jesus. God wants us to, and we need to, develop a vehement hatred for sin in our lives. When we realize how much we have been forgiven, we will love Jesus more. When love is perfected, sin will cease.

Chapter 15

Famous Last Words

At the end of Jesus' public ministry, He prayed one last prayer for His disciples. This is the prayer we touched on earlier, recorded in the seventeenth chapter of John. In the final seventeen verses of this prayer, Jesus prays five times that we would be one. He first asked Our Father to keep us, through His name, so that we can be one. Having God revealed to us as our Father, unites us as part of the Family of God. Having Him as "Savior" unites us through Jesus. As Jesus continues His prayer, He asks that joy be fulfilled in His disciples through this unity and the word He had preached to them in spite of the persecution they would have to endure. He then prays that we not be taken out of the world but be kept from evil. After this, He prays that we would be sanctified. He then includes us in this prayer. He prays three times that we would be one and the fourth that we will be made perfect in one. Paul clarifies two things. In First Corinthians 12 he says,

> "For by one Spirit are we all baptized into one body, whether we be Jews or Gentiles, whether we be bond or free; and have been

all made to drink into one Spirit. For the body is not one member, but many. If the foot shall say, Because I am not the hand, I am not of the body; is it therefore not of the body? And if the ear shall say, Because I am not the eye, I am not of the body; is it therefore not of the body? If the whole body were an eye, where were the hearing? If the whole were hearing, where were the smelling?"

Because we know in part, regardless of how good our church doctrine is, we cannot fully represent Christ as individual fragments of His shattered body. It is only through unity we can reveal a complete picture of Christ to the world. In Ephesians 4, Paul reveals a second thing,

"And he gave some, apostles; and some, prophets; and some, evangelists; and some, pastors and teachers; for the perfecting of the saints, for the work of the ministry, for the edifying of the body of Christ: till we all come in the unity of the faith, and of the knowledge of the Son of God, unto a perfect man, unto the measure of the stature of the fulness of Christ:... speaking

the truth in love, may grow up into him in
all things, which is the head, even Christ."

We require both unity of faith and knowledge of
Jesus to fulfill our destinies. This unity is found first
in our intimacy with Christ. When we will unite
with Jesus in His prayer, we enter into an intimate
relationship with Him as well as all the other
believers who are doing the same. As we do this
faithfully, both our knowledge of Jesus and our
faith will increase. This last prayer of His public
ministry revealed His greatest desire. He wants
more than anything for us to be one. Jesus
teaches us to pray "Our Father." In Luke Jesus told
us to say His prayer with Him daily. In Matthew He
taught us how to pray it from our hearts. Jesus
wants us to unite with Him.

Immediately after this, Jesus went into the Garden
of Gethsemane. As Jesus entered the Garden, He
left most of His disciples in one place and took
Peter, James and John a little farther with Him. He
asked them to watch and pray that they would not
enter into temptation. He separated Himself from
them and prayed earnestly that   a "cup" might
pass from Him. Jesus prayed this three times and
returned to His disciples after each. Two times
Jesus admonished them to pray they would not

enter into temptation. The final time He returned and told them to sleep on.

The writers of the first three Gospels made no attempt to explain what Jesus was referring to by "this cup". They may either have thought the nature of the cup was obvious or they may not have been sure of its meaning. Whatever their reason, I'm about to fall into the trap they avoided. I'm offering my opinion because, whether I'm right or wrong, I believe I have received benefit from believing it.

I don't think Jesus is trying to find a way to save mankind without dying. He had already rejected one when He was tempted in the wilderness. He knew He had to die. He had been telling His apostles that He had to die and be raised again the third day. It just doesn't make sense to me that He would be asking the Father over and over for an alternative plan. I don't think He was praying to not bear the sins of the world. He knew He would have to do that even before John the Baptist said, "Behold the Lamb of God." I don't think He was praying not to be forsaken by His Father. His question, from the cross, "Why hast Thou forsaken me?" is not ingenuous. What else is there?

Jesus knew the wages of sin. All Jesus had to do was to die for our sins. He didn't have to suffer as much as He did for our sins to be forgiven. I believe the "cup", Jesus prayed about, is the horrendous suffering that accompanied His death. Jesus has always known our thinking about sin has to change.

> Romans 12:2 "And be not conformed to this world: but be ye transformed by the renewing of your mind, that ye may prove what is that good, and acceptable, and perfect, will of God."

The metamorphosis that changes us from fallen sons of Adam to the image of the Son of God requires our thinking to be totally changed with regard to sin. I believe, as Jesus prayed for some other way to be found to change our minds about sin, His Father took Him back to His disciples. Instead of praying not to enter into temptation, they slept. Today, most of the Church thinks it's OK to be tempted. We are still asleep. In the Garden Jesus did more than volunteer to die for our sins. He volunteered to suffer the most horrendous death to show us the ravages of sin. He prayed, till the sweat fell as drops of blood three times, that we would wake up and spare Him that suffering.

Yet we sleep on. As long as we desire evil things (are tempted) and think everything is OK, we continue to sleep. As I meditate on the suffering Jesus went through, I see many correlations to what sin does to us as believers. God is using this in my life to lead me "not into temptation." It is part of my metamorphosis. I strongly recommend we all allow this, tremendous sacrifice and suffering of Jesus, to be a focal point in our daily meditations. When our thinking is totally renewed, our lives will be transformed. We will see sin as God sees sin.

A long time ago I had a daughter that was going through a really difficult time in her life. She was in rebellion and totally out of control. She asked me a question. "Why do you hate me?" I never hated my daughter. I love all my children very much. I told her, "Because you murdered my little girl." I believe this is a little similar to how God views us. It explains how God can love sinners and hate sin. My daughter was killing herself with everything she did. I could see that but she couldn't. God sees that our sin is destroying us. It is not doing it quickly or mercifully. It is killing us slowly with unnoticed horror and suffering. If we see sin in our lives as God sees it, we would have to be totally insane to want to sin. God has not given us a spirit

of fear. He has given us power and love through
His Holy Spirit and a renewed sound mind.

Chapter 16

Truth is Not on a Ballot

When I was teaching journeymen electricians, I would sometimes ask them a question, "Does electricity always follow the path of least resistance?" the answer was almost always unanimously "yes". I would then explain, "If electricity follows the path of least resistance only the first light on a circuit would come on. Instantly a light came on. They realized they all believed a lie. In Matthew chapter 7 Jesus tells us, "Enter ye in at the strait gate: for wide is the gate, and broad is the way, that leadeth to destruction, and many there be which go in thereat: because strait is the gate, and narrow is the way, which leadeth unto life, and few there be that find it." In spite of everything God has done, most people are on the wrong road to the wrong place. For some reason, we seem to be more susceptible to lies than to truth.

The same church that taught me, "It's not what you know, it is who you know" rejected me. When they asked me to become an elder, I gave them a list of "paraphrased" scriptures I believed in. As soon as they read the list, they told me I could not be an elder if I believed those things. I met one of the elders a couple of days later. He told me he realized what I had done and he seemed genuinely embarrassed because they didn't believe those scriptures. J. B. Phillips, in his translation of the New Testament, changes a passage to what he (thinks it should say) because he doesn't understand it. In a footnote he says "...A slip of the pen on the part of Paul or ...copyist's error". Nearly every modern translation has changed one little word in Galatians 2:20 from King James "I live by the faith *of* the Son of God" to "in". Perhaps the majority opinion is correct for them, but I know that if I depend on my faith, I will fail utterly. If I depend on Jesus' faith, He will fulfill my destiny. A belief that electricity always follows the path of least resistance can work quite well for some things. It can also kill you. Whether a view is held by the majority or minority does not make it true. The problem with the majority view, when it's wrong, is it becomes convincing. A lie repeated often enough becomes accepted as truth.

Jesus always was and always will be the Truth. We are promised that if we seek Him we will find Him. Jesus gives us faith and the trying of our faith produces hope that enables us to endure to the prize. It is essential that we first believe the "prize" is attainable. Most of the time, we only realize, the impossibility of attaining the "prize". We forget that God can do all things possible and impossible. If we don't believe God can perfect us here and now, our destinies will never be fulfilled in our lifetimes. If we don't believe the gifts of the Holy Spirit are available to us today, we will never receive them. If we don't believe the Holy Spirit will produce fruit in our lives, He probably won't. If we don't believe salvation is available to everyone, we won't offer it to them. If we say we don't believe something, we better not need it or want it, because we won't get it. Love believes all things.

Paul said some interesting things to the Corinthians. First Corinthians 12:25, 26 say, "God hath tempered the body together, having given more abundant honour to that part which lacked: that there should be no schism in the body; but that the members should have the same care one for another." It seems that churches may have divided because they've overlooked the fact that God has given more abundant honor to the parts of His body that lack. I'm sure that each side of a divisive argument thinks the other side is lacking. Paul tells us we should have the same care (more abundant honor) for one another.

Paul goes on to ask several questions. Among these questions, are two in particular, "Are all prophets?" and "Do all speak with tongues? ". The apparent answer to these questions is "no". In chapter 14 Paul says, "I would that ye all spake with tongues, but rather that ye prophesied." God desires everyone to be saved. He desires each of us to fulfill our destiny. Most people neglect the great salvation God has made available to each of us. Through Paul, God revealed that He not only wants everyone to, at least, speak in tongues; He prefers we all prophesy. It makes no sense for God to want everyone to have something and not make it available to them. This principle is true universally. Everything God wants us to have is available. If God hadn't made it available, it would prove He did not want us to have it and make Him a liar. Like the early disciples, we far too often think, because something is impossible, it's not available. It's only when we realize that every part of our Christian life is impossible, we become totally dependent on the One for whom all things are possible. Just because things are impossible, doesn't mean they are hopeless. Through hope (enduring faith) all things are possible.

Believing things are inaccessible, is only one of the half-truths Satan is using to cripple the Church. For various reasons, most of us fall under his spell from time to time. Most of the time, I believe his half-truths because they make me feel better about myself or help me to be less of an outcast from the world. Because sin is horrible, unforgivable rebellion against God, instead of feeling the magnitude of true remorse, we like to believe half-truths about it. We say sin is merely missing the mark. We believe all we have to do is gleefully admit our sins and because Jesus is faithful and just, He forgives our sins and removes all consequence. We believe God has made the sinless life He commands us to live inaccessible merely because it's impossible. Each of these lies from hell is a half-truth. These are the devils specialties. I'm sure most of us are tender hearted enough to understand what I've just said. I pray your indulgence as I proceed to explain these lies more clearly for the rest of us.

Using the root origin of a word is not always a reliable key to its definition. A cool fire may be very hot in spite of the origin of the word cool. Modern theologians overuse root origins to define terms. We usually create a new word because the old root words fail to completely convey our intended thought. Root words may hint at the meaning but they rarely define the new term. In the case of sin, we see **miss the mark** emphasized from its root. Its root also implies a failure or inability to partake of the spoils of war. Sin is probably more closely related to desertion during a military campaign than not hitting the target. It's easy to miss the mark when you're running the wrong way. If our mark is the finish line of a race we will never win the prize by running the wrong direction. If we confess the truth, Jesus will forgive us and turn us around so that we can run in the right direction. The consequences of sin are so terrible that God will destroy both heaven and earth. The damage we cause by sin is irreparable to the point that God will have to destroy this earth and create a new one.

I have a lot more things I would like to say. I believe there would be no end to my writing of books. Indeed if I continue it would be "weariness in the flesh". I want to leave you in better hands than mine. I know in part, but there is One who is Truth. Jesus tells us in John the 16th chapter, "Howbeit when he, the Spirit of truth, is come, he will guide you into all truth." I hope to see you on the other side. Until then let us pray and meditate together and with Jesus daily, "Our Father which art in heaven, Hallowed be thy name. Thy kingdom come. Thy will be done in earth, as it is in heaven.

Give us this day our daily bread. And forgive us our debts, as we forgive our debtors. And lead us not into temptation, but deliver us from evil: For thine is the kingdom, and the power, and the glory, for ever. Amen."